POETRY

is the

PORTAL

KARY OBERBRUNNER

Published by Ethos Collective™
PO Box 43, Powell, OH 43065
www.ethoscollective.vip

LCCN: 2023900304
Paperback ISBN: 978-1-63680-116-2
Hardcover ISBN: 978-1-63680-117-9
e-book ISBN: 978-1-63680-118-6

Available in paperback, hardcover, e-book, and audiobook

You snap
pictures of
the sunset
and forget
you're more
beautiful
than the sky.

Loving you
is the only crazy,
I ever want.

All our
jagged
differences
fade
into
one
smooth
paradox
when our
bodies
tangle
together.

Froth and foam, your mind the forbidden drink. I risk certainty and bet ignorance for a chance encounter we might mix our magic.

You command
a room
without effort.
But I see
beneath your
skin.

You entrust
me with your
emotions and I
vow to guard
them well.

Time no longer
has meaning when
my mind makes
love with yours.

You
stirred
beside me
while I
dreamed.

I stayed
asleep
fearing,
you were
my make
believe.

Poetry is the prescription God used to save my soul.

I SPENT
YEARS
TRYING
TO TAME
OTHERS,
UNTIL I MET
YOU—MY
WILD.

When I met you my performance ended.
The audience lost meaning.
The applause rang hollow.
Rewriting a new script with you
is the only option that makes perfect sense,
despite the insanity of it all.

When you cry,
something ignites me
and I'd give anything
to take your tears.

The idea of what
could be with you,
erases the fear of
what might be
without you.

Your laughter
is proof I will
love again
someday.

WHEN YOU
DON'T
THINK I'M
WATCHING,
IN THOSE
MOMENTS,
I'M MOST
CAPTIVATED
BY YOUR
BEAUTY.

In my mind,
we are lovers.

In my body,
we are strangers.

In my soul,
we are friends.

WHEN YOU
WALKED INTO
MY LIFE, THE
PRESSURE TO
PERFORM LEFT
THE BUILDING.

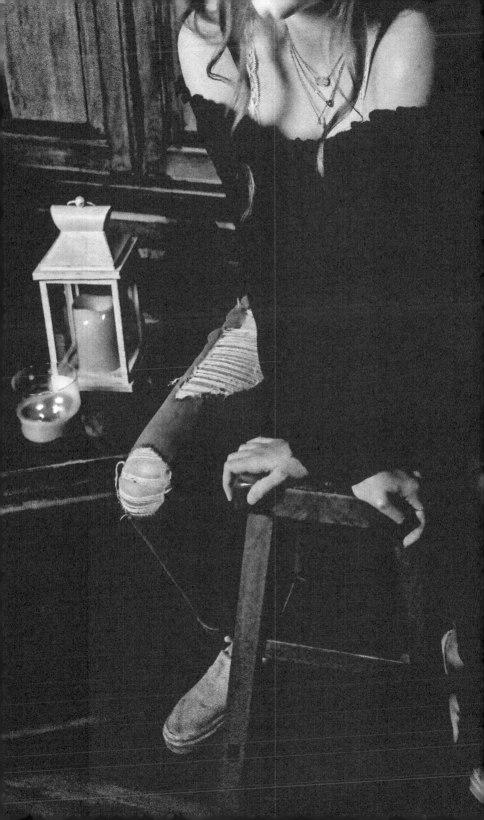

effortless afternoons never
tempted me, until you did.

In a world
where you
didn't exist,
keeping score
always made
sense.

But now I
know you're
real, the only
win is us
together.

Your love
is the only
medicine
that can
heal my
troubled
soul.

Before I met you
I was haunted by
the idea of your
existence.

Now that I know
you're real, I'm only
haunted by the idea
of your departure.

Your lips cannot lie,
holding you in my
soak-skinned arms.

Our new adventure
etched in eternity while
we take on the world.

My life was
predictable
before you.

Now it's a wild
storm and I
wouldn't want it
any other way.

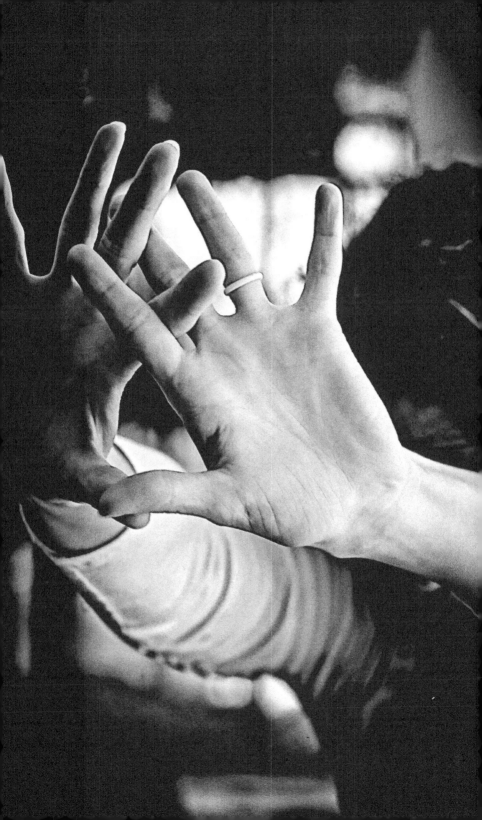

Sun-kissed
mornings.

Gently
swinging
hammocks.

Undiscovered
adventures.

You've
helped me
remember a
forgotten
beautiful.

I used to
distract
my days
pretending
I needed
to save the
world.

Then I met
you, found
a new
world, and
realized
I was the
one in need
of saving.

You'll never
know how
much space
you take up
inside my
head.

You're the only
interruption I
welcome any
day of the week.

I'd trade
forever to
drink you
deep into
my soul.

Your laughter is
confidence and
comfort wrapped
into one.

A smile on
your sun-
kissed face,
lights up even
the gloomiest
of days.

I look within and see my heart on fire,
set ablaze by the idea of us.

With you in my arms,
I can face whatever
cruelty the world
throws my way.

I find eternity
in your eyes and
gladly welcome
our new forever.

When life fails
to live up to the
hype, you still
come through
as my constant.

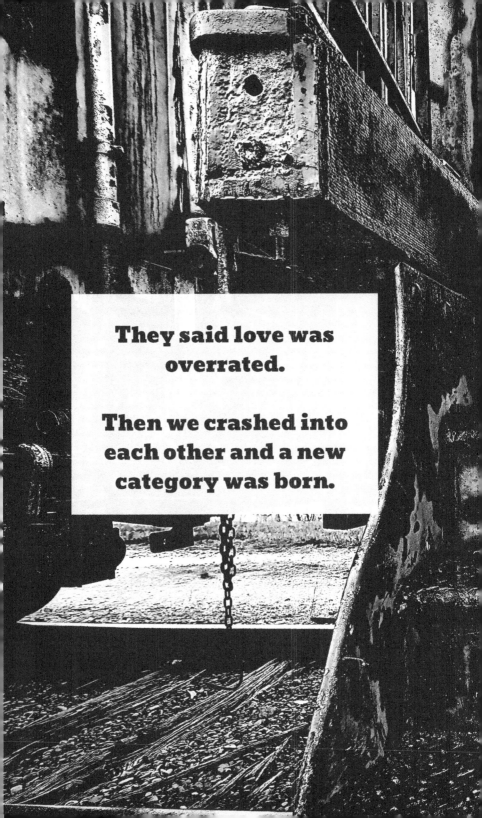

They said love was overrated.

Then we crashed into each other and a new category was born.

WEALTH AND FAME FADE IN LIGHT OF A SIMPLE LIFE WITH YOU.

When I stopped
defending and
started listening,
I realized we're
not as separate as
I once imagined.

*Your perspective
seasons my ordinary days.*

OUR HEARTS
TWISTED
TOGETHER,

NO LONGER
A CHANCE
OF ESCAPING
ALIVE.

Dogmatic
and alone.

Compromise
and together.

This choice
challenges
the best of us
and saves the
worst of us.

Your ideas a liquid conversation, poured out before me, an irresistible elixir, coaxing the loneliest to surrender independence.

Crisp leaves collect
memories in my mind,
blowing dreams of
yesterday, through our
new bigger future.

Your drops of Saturn,
offer comfort and
warmth on a cold,
otherwise forgettable,
September day.

No more borders or
boundaries hold the
line that caged my
fire before I met you.

Liberated flames
dance dangerously
close to the idea of us,
released into the wild.

Affirmation from others, an inferior alternative, to our afternoon at sea, my preferred reality.

A familiar song
I can't quite recall.

Our chance encounter
reminds me
we've met before.

In a daydream
or a nightmare.

Time won't lie.

Until then, I'll rest
in your arms.

Unleashed
emotions
might
betray
me, but
you're a
risk
worth
taking.

Inspiration
drips down
as I behold
beauty from
inside you.

Poetry is the portal, imagination the escape.

After dinner plans lose
their meaning when I get
lost inside your wonder.

My
restless
heart, a
desperate
plight,
until I
found my
peace
within
your
presence.

LACE AND
SATIN FOREVER
OUTLAWED,
WHEN YOU
WORE THEM
WELL.

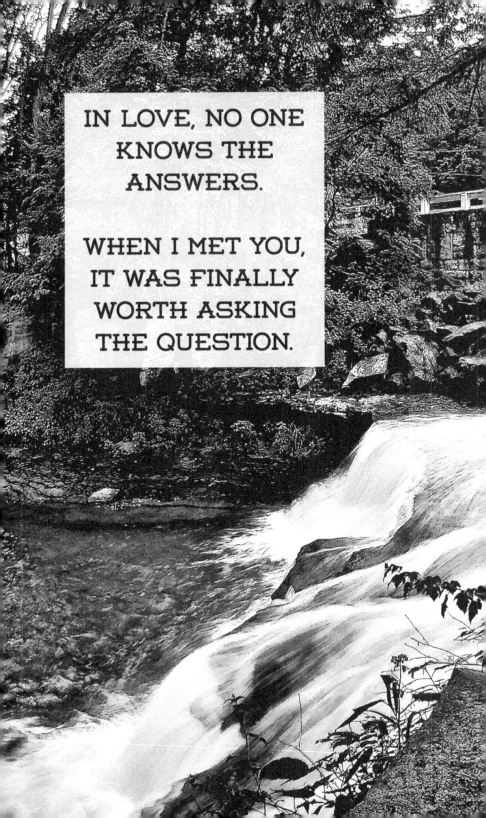

Others see a warrior.
I know an angel.

Before you
I grew tired
with silly
games of
love and loss.

But you've
made play
simple and
love easy.

Your love makes
lying in bed
under covers,
my new favorite
pastime.

A violent storm
next to you, more
appealing than a
peaceful afternoon
without you.

The cozy way you decorate my heart gives me safety to nap in the middle of a storm.

I drop my
sword when
our minds
meet in new
places.

Your stories
make me smile.

My heart can
finally be still.

Our love is catastrophic.
It's meant to be.
Something called
chemistry.

Before you, death couldn't
come fast enough.

After you, I'll never live
long enough.

Oil and water have
a better chance of
blending together,
than me making it a
day without your love.

I had little money
when we met.

You loved me
nonetheless.

Today, wealth
comes easy.

But your love is
most valuable of all.

"Let him go," the wise woman told her.

"You can't receive the next gift, still holding a heart full of hurt."

He never opened up his heart again. The cost of losing someone else was a price he wouldn't pay.

Getting
kissed, she
dreamed
of another.

Together
with the
wrong
one, was
better
than alone
with the
right one.

He worries what he'll say when he meets her. If he only knew, she already loves him.

You're my new kind of effortless, an unforeseen friendship, light and right wrapped into one.

If you knew how much I dreamed of you, my words would be enough.

SHE HID PERFECTLY IN
PLAIN SIGHT WHILE HE
WAITED FOR AN
IMPERFECT LOVE.

He wasn't confident.
He just knew she was worth the risk.

She couldn't settle as long as he existed, even if only in memories.

She saw his heart.

He saw her mind.

Poisoned pasts
couldn't
extinguish their
bigger future.

Shaky souls lit
a new fire and
basked in the
warmth of a
novel idea.

"Convince me
you're not in
love," one friend
said to another.

"Convince me I
am," the other
replied back.

"That's simple.
I'll confess my
love to her,
while you watch
and worry."

We do strange
things in love.
Ignoring those
we want and
paying
attention to
those we don't.

she knew
she wanted
him,
watching
the way he
cared for
those who
could never
repay.

He vowed to never love,
leaving drama at the door.

But a stranger resolved
to keep knocking and he
dared to believe again.

I closed my storybook until your love opened it again.

Let the world burn,
as long I'm beside you.

Immune to love, she
resolved to stay inside.

He felt her ice, but
honored from a
distance.

When he fell sick, she
missed his warmth and
went searching.

He left this world and
now she's alone,
wondering how it
might have been.

You wouldn't be
happy if she
changed.

And yet you
spend a lifetime
trying, rather
than a moment
loving.

He didn't know she was
watching.

She didn't know he cared.

Get on with confessions.

If life ended tonight they'd
both die with regret.

The perfect day is an imperfect one, as long as you're in it.

You're the movie
I wish I was making.

The book
I wish I was reading.

The sunset
I wish I was seeing.

I'll get
lost in
any
moment
as long
as I'm
with you.

Your mind,
a complex
mystery, worth
undressing.

Let those
ghosts die,
vampires
sent to suck
your beauty.

You're far
too valuable
to entertain
their
madness.

We don't make sense on paper. Then again my heart never cared.

On a summer
night I fell upon
your words and
understood their
meaning.

Divine visitors
dispatched
lifetimes ago.

In a moment,
my rebirth,
our new reality.

She never noticed
until he stopped
noticing.

She never believed
until he stopped
believing.

Will she return the
favor or run forever?

This is the storyline
of our stars.

SOME WANT SIMPLE.
BUT FOR SOME
REASON, I'M
CAUGHT IN YOUR
BEAUTIFUL CHAOS.

I met you in a movie,
but thought you
were a dream.

You hijacked my
heart, until I saw
you on the street.

Now that I know you
exist, I'm uncertain
about disrupting the
ideal. I'm too scared I
won't measure up.

A forgotten forest,
lip-locked by freshly
fallen snow.

Our heartbeats the
only sound.

Proof we're not
only dreaming.

The fight to be
right faded
when I realized
life without
you felt wrong.

I knew you were the one when
I undressed my soul and you
stayed anyways.

In your eyes my new universe is born.

I walked into
the room,
heard our
song, and then
remembered
we hadn't met.

Something tells
me risking love
with you is the
safest bet I'll
ever make.

I
craved
the
grey,
but
your
colors
somehow
found
a
way
inside.

To Grandma Millie
You felt the darkness of my teenage poetry and
believed one day I would find the light.

I did.

Mildred F. Oberbrunner
1932-2022

Special Thanks

Photographers

Mark and Shelly Thomas

You are both incredible photographers.
You've added so much value to me and my businesses.
I love Mark and Shelly Photography.
MarkAndShellyPhotography.Art

Models

I am blessed by your trust and belief in this project.

Lena Morgan
Renee Vidor
Brandi Mae
Sarah Grandstaff
Cassidy Smith
Michelle Waugh Brinkley
Jeff Davidson and Cassie Bladen
Natalie Hanson
Kara and Andrew Valentine
Michelle Weidenbenner
Gisele Wyne
Chris and Amanda Lexow
Kiera Colson

Made in the USA
Monee, IL
19 January 2023

25639333R00116